# The Naked I: Insides Out

Created by 20% Theatre Company Twin Cities
with the contributions of 25 queer
and transgender writers and allies.

World Premiere: February 13-23, 2014
at Intermedia Arts in Minneapolis, MN.

Inspired by
*The Naked I: Monologues From Beyond The Binary*,
by Tobias K. Davis,
and following
*The Naked I: Wide Open*,
created by 20% Theatre Company in 2012.

www.tctwentypercent.org

Front Cover Illustration by Anna Bongiovanni (www.annabongiovanni.com).
Cover and Interior Layout by Alyx J. Hanson (www.alyxjhanson.com).
Edited by Claire Avitabile and Alyx J. Hanson.

## Notes on Character:

This Play can be performed by as few as seven actors, to as many as 30 or more. Ideally, performers will represent gender identities as diverse as the characters in the Play do, but by no means is it necessary for a performer to identify the same as a character they are portraying.

## Notes on Staging:

*The Naked I: Insides Out* was created with minimalism in mind – no fancy sets or costumes here, just a few chairs and props as needed. All that matters are the stories, and the individuals telling them. These pieces can – and should – be performed not only in conventional theatre venues, but unconventional ones as well – such as schools, coffee shops, business establishments, churches, etc.

Stage directions are present merely to serve as a guide, or to share how a piece was staged in the world premiere. Producers should in no way feel they have to follow any of the stage directions.

## Acknowledgements:

20% Theatre Company Twin Cities would like thank all of the writers, directors, performers, designers, stage managers, production assistants, interns, company members, board members, donors, sponsors, and volunteers who helped make the world premiere of *The Naked I: Insides Out* possible.

In addition to those 100+ beautiful artists and contributors, enormous thanks to Tobias K. Davis, Jake Davis and Intermedia Arts, Madame of the Arts, Metropolitan Regional Arts Council, the Carolyn Foundation, and Minneapolis Public Libraries.

# ACT ONE

## WHAT IT'S LIKE
*by Christopher Soden and Claire Avitabile*

*An empty stage full of gorgeous queer bodies. This group should be as diverse as possible – with regards to race, age, size, ability, and gender identity. Written for 7 people but could be expanded – preferably not more than 9 or 10 people.*

| | |
|---|---|
| ONE: | You don't know what it's like |
| SEVEN: | To hear whispers |
| TWO: | Snickers |
| THREE: | Giggles |
| FOUR: | When you enter a room |
| FIVE: | Or leave one. |

| | |
|---|---|
| THREE: | You don't know what it's like |
| SIX: | When they stare with such confusion |
| SEVEN : | Like you're from another planet |

| | |
|---|---|
| TWO: | When strangers walk up and spit in your hair |
| THREE: | Stalk you like some pitiful beast |

| | |
|---|---|
| SIX: | Cross the street so they don't have to walk by you |
| FIVE: | Or wait for you in shadows |
| ONE: | Look you up and down like you don't belong |
| FIVE: | Like you shouldn't be in this store |
| SIX: | Or eating at this restaurant |
| SEVEN: | Or drinking at this bar |
| THREE: | Or dancing in this club |
| FOUR: | Or sitting on this bench |
| SIX: | Or headed to work on this bus. |
| | |
| SEVEN: | You don't know what it's like, when they move in real close, pretend to want you, pretend to care, pretend to be interested |
| FIVE: | Just so they can tokenize you |
| TWO: | So they can study you, like a science experiment |
| SIX: | So they can try to break you. |
| | |
| ONE: | You don't know what it's like when your father |
| SIX: | Your mother |
| FOUR: | Your brother |
| TWO: | Your best friend |

| | |
|---|---|
| SEVEN: | Your teacher |
| SIX: | Your minister |
| THREE: | Your boss says: |
| FIVE: | "You're not really a boy" |
| ONE: | "You're not a real woman" |
| TWO: | That you could never be a woman |
| FOUR: | That you just don't make any sense |
| SIX: | "What's wrong with you?" |
| TWO: | "I don't want to know." |
| ONE: | "Why can't you just be normal?" |

| | |
|---|---|
| THREE: | You don't know what it's like |
| SEVEN: | To do a cartwheel followed by a somersault followed by wishing so hard you could fold your hands into a pistol and no longer exist. |
| FIVE: | You don't know what it's like |
| SIX: | To be pushed, kicked, beaten, |
| ONE: | Tied down, raped, |
| FOUR: | Or killed |
| *(pause)* | |
| TWO: | For just being who you are. |

| | |
|---|---|
| SIX: | For so long I asked myself: |
| ALL : | "What did I do?" |

| | |
|---|---|
| SEVEN: | You don't know what it's like |
| THREE: | To be called |
| ONE: | "disgusting" |
| TWO: | To be called |
| FIVE: | "a mistake that Mother Nature made" |
| FOUR: | To be told |
| SIX: | "you will never fit in" |
| SEVEN: | To be told |
| THREE: | "nobody will ever love you like that." |

(*pause - transition*)

| | |
|---|---|
| ONE: | Actually – *(looking around the audience)* I think many of you probably do know what it's like. You know damn well what it's like. You've been the butt of a joke. You've been misgendered, ignored, discriminated against, even attacked, and none of this is okay. |
| TWO: | But you know what else? |
| THREE: | You are loved. WE are fucking loved. |
| FOUR: | And we do fit in. |
| ONE: | And we are NOT fucking mistakes. |

| | |
|---|---|
| FIVE: | I am fucking GORGEOUS and I belong anywhere I want to be. |
| FOUR: | We have come so far – as a queer community – as a society – generations and generations of fighters and pain and struggle and triumph and BEAUTY! |
| FIVE: | But this journey is far from over, and there is so much left to do. |
| THREE: | So much more to fight for. To strive for. |
| SIX: | To live for. |
| TWO: | So let's kick off the dirt and keep working. |
| SIX: | Let's no longer tolerate *not being tolerated.* |
| ONE: | Let's keep dreaming... |
| SEVEN: | Let's keep educating and talking and listening – and not just to people outside of our community, but also to our friends and lovers and family, because we, too, are guilty of our own phobias and misunderstandings and assumptions (I know you know what I'm talking about...) and we need to remember to speak up for ourselves even in the places we call home. |
| FOUR: | Movement leads to momentum |
| FIVE: | And momentum leads to change. |
| TWO: | So let's keep moving. |
| ALL: | Are you with us? |

# CORPOREOSARTORIAPHOBIA
*by Cat Hammond*

*At the beginning of the piece, the performer should be wearing all of the "looks" listed below, layered one on top of the other, such that they can remove each look to reveal the one beneath it. After each section, the clothes from the previous look should be removed and tossed onto the stage.*

*Look 1: Sweatpants and Extra Large Grey Sweatshirt*
This is me at my 9 am class.
I wore sweatpants and a baggy sweatshirt
because I was running late.
It's a theatre class—I can get away with it, right?
We might be doing movement work, right?
Nope.
I look frumpy and shapeless. No, worse—
those words are for women—
I look like a slob.
Did you ever hear of a girl slob?
Me either.

*Look 2: Casual Rumpled Skirt and Sweatshirt*
Well, at least now I've graduated to frumpy and shapeless.
This is me trying to figure out how to wear the skirt
I bought at the thrift store last week.
I liked the look of it—
but what goes with it?
You know,
I've seen thousands of people wearing skirts in my life,
and this one's not particularly unusual,
so why does a decent outfit remain so elusive?
I've got to pay closer attention.
Well, nothing I own is working.
That's for sure.
Guess it's back to the drawing board
And the thrift store.

*Look 3: Black Dress and Black Flower Hair Clip*
This is me on my way to the opera.

I have sworn off male dress clothes for good.
Ill-fitting button-down shirts
Clunky shoes and sturdy belts
Slacks
It's impossible to say whether I hate the clothes because they all scream "masculine"
Or whether I hate being masculine because of how terrible I look when I dress the part.
*(applying lipstick)*
I'm not a woman trapped in a man's body...
I'm a person who just wants to be pretty
Trapped in a society where only women are pretty.

*Look 4: Ill-fitting T-Shirt and Jeans*
This is me in class again.
Today I wasn't running late—
until I opened my closet door.
And realized:
It's too cold outside for a skirt...
I wore that sweater last week...
I have no matching socks clean??
I am so sick of these jeans.
This shirt won't work with anything else...
My shoes are filthy.
Shit, I have to go.
Fuck, my hair.
I don't have time to dry it.
It'll be frizzy
And hang down straight again
And I'll look like a douchebag pothead
Again.
Not that the wind doesn't do that anyway
No matter how much attention I give it before I leave.
I have to go.
...Fuck!

*Look 5: T-Shirt and Khaki Shorts*
*(with gradually mounting frustration)*
This is me in the summer
Trying out short shorts for the first time.
How do I look? The mirror is silent and inscrutable.

I've shaved off my leg hair,
but an even thicker layer of insecurity remains—
How do I look?
By now it is impossible to separate
my body issues from my fashion sense
(if I have any)
from everyone else's sense
of how these clothes should be worn
and by whom.
Ok, so my thighs are kind of pudgy
and muscular
and pale
But are they really disgustingly so?
Or do I just think so?
Or should I even care at all?
*(Tearing off shirt and shorts)*
How do I look? How do I look?!

*Look 6: Plain Low-Rise Briefs*
*(peacefully)*
This is me.
Hairy legs and all, this is me.
White skin and all, this is me.
Deep voice and all, big feet and all, this is me
And, no matter how much I wish sometimes,
there's simply no escaping that. No—

This is me.

*(plucks flower hair clip from among the scattered clothing
and affixes it to hair; smiling)*

Or at least, it's what I've got to work with.

# I SHOOK
*by Suzi Gard*

I shook
When I finally decided to come out to my family.
Would you believe that it was a Yogi tea bag that finally shook
me out of the closet?
It's a long story. Let's rewind first.

She's a young girl of seven: high-dive brave, bendy backed and
wide eyed. And she is full of queer little thoughts in her queer
little head. Her queer little body is shaking, shaking, shaking
with queer little feelings that you just don't bring up at the
dinner table. While her family's heads bow to pray, her head
bows to study the curious curve in the valley of her lap.
And her queer little head buzzes:
Oh, what beautiful bodies we have!
...to keep covered up, wrapped up, tied, laced, and knotted.

"Kelsey Purdue, she's got flaming red hair! Oh she's so sweet,
so funny, sometimes I just want to kiss her!"
Dad said, "Don't let anyone else hear you say that."
I stopped telling Dad about my friends after that.
The next day I played kissing games with the blonde twin
neighbor girls in their bedroom closet.
"Mommy, can a man marry a man?
Mommy, can I join wrestling?
Mommy, what is this called?"
*(touching, gesturing toward vulva)*

FAST FORWARD FIVE YEARS.

This body—I'm not ready for this body.
This body that is so bumpy, curvy, hungry, unruly, fickle,
freckled, and temperamental,
this body so wanted by others and unwanted by me.
When I was twelve I counted my ribs like rungs on Jacob's
ladder and prayed for more,
always short on my stairway to heaven.
It took me two years to realize that there are already

**9**

constellations on my skin,
and galaxies in my eyes and that pick up sticks is not a game a
father wants to play with his child's body
when legs like twigs
buckle under the weight of budding breasts.
I plucked the roses from my own cheeks.
At age fourteen, the dam burst forth
and armies of hormones flooded my veins.
I felt every budding thought
in my queer little head blossom into forbidden fruit.
Oh Sarah! Oh Sadie! Oh Hannah! Oh Jess! Oh man, I like girls!

He shook
When he kissed his best friend, me, for the first time.
And my still virginal, curious, sex-starved teenage self said,
Should I fuck him?
I shouldn't fuck him. He's my best friend.
I don't even know if I like...that.
Maybe I should fuck him. No, I shouldn't fuck him.
We fucked.
We fucked.
We dated.
We almost got engaged.

But I shook
Coming down from that first time with her.

I am...I am...I am....a single word caught in the throats of
generations of people who suffered in their own misnamed
flesh and in their own condemned blood and will never see
their own flesh and blood come into the world. The only way
you can bring them to life is to dislodge that word that seems
to determine your public worth. I know what I deserve. And
though I may only be a sheet of paper on a legislator's desk, I
am...I am a human shaking before you.

I shook in my dark Minneapolis apartment, making tea,
My family surrounded me with concerned eyes and knitted
brows, wondering why I shook. And as I tore open that little
tea packet, I read that seldom helpful, vaguely inspirational
phrase on the paper tab:

BE PROUD OF WHO YOU ARE.

Be proud of who you are!
Do not apologize for the space you take or the love you make.
Never apologize, because
I will not apologize for my wild heart.
I will not apologize for the
untamable little hairs my body makes.
I will not apologize for the blood of my sex.
I will not apologize for the way you read my body's story.
I will not apologize for the flesh that pillows my lover's head.
I will not apologize for the eyesore
of my generation's struggle on your TV screen.

And though it may burn you
to hold a secret that causes you to shake
Like I shook
Remember that every verse you write, every note you pluck,
every muscle you awaken, every etch you carve, every line you
spit, is a declaration, a liberation, a celebration of self.

I'm here. I love. I feel. I need. I am. I am. I am. *(pound chest like heartbeat)* X∞

QUEER.

## MAN-ISH
*by Ben Masters*

It took six months of dating to learn that I was in a same-gender relationship.

The epiphany came as my boyfriend and I were filling out an audience survey after an amazing play we'd seen. I wanted to show my appreciation and give my feedback. But how would I answer that first question: What is your gender identity?

There was plenty of blank space to fill, and, thankfully, no aggravating boxes to check. Still, I jiggled my pencil, hoping that the right words would fall out onto the page.

I thought back to a gender identity spectrum that I had seen in countless presentations, how I wished I could put a name to the gender a few points down the line from "man." Brow scrunched, I scribbled down my attempt.

After I finished with the survey, I leaned over to see what my boyfriend had written. And there, at the top of the page, next to "gender identity" I saw: "man" hyphen "ish". Man-ish.

In excitement I pointed at his survey and brandished mine. "Look!" I said. "Look! We're both man-ish!"

Yes, I know it's a little silly. But still I like the idea of the two of us — two man-ish queers — discovering after half a year that we really were in a same-gender relationship.

# KNOCK ON WOOD
*by Leslie Lagerstrom*

*Lights up on Leslie, a cisgender mother, mid-30s to mid 40s.*

I can't remember exactly when it became my mantra, but somewhere along the line I abandoned all reason, turned my back on logic, and succumbed to superstition. The kind of superstition learned on the playgrounds of my childhood, where chanting a particular phrase would make everything all better, or protect you from harm, depending on your situation.

"Circle, circle. Dot, dot. Now you have the cooties shot."
If only it was that simple.

"Find a penny pick it up all the day you'll have good luck."
That one always seemed to work — as long as you found a penny.

As a mom of a transgender child, I found the need to reach deep into this medicine cabinet of protective sayings. To rely upon the prescription strength that came with that simple, yet all-encompassing verbal immunization: Knock on wood.

Learning that our child was transgender, I found myself transformed from a rational human being, to a mother fraught with worry. An all too common state of being, I quickly learned, for parents like me whose children knew at an unusually young age, that there was a disconnect between their mind and body. And so I adopted that familiar incantation from my youth, using it on a daily basis as an insurance policy for the worries and fears I had for Sam that were accidentally spoken out loud.

In the early days it went something like this...

I've read the research studies that have found only 2% of gender variant kids actually go on to be transgender. What are the chances Sam will fall into that category?

*Knock on wood.*

Just because she insists on getting the boy's Happy Meal toy doesn't mean she really thinks she is a boy.

*Knock on wood.*

They didn't intend to exclude Sam from the birthday party. Those parents could not be that cruel to an eight year-old child, could they?

*Knock on wood.*

It doesn't mean anything that she wants to wear boy's Super Hero underpants.

*Knock on wood.*

Those classmates will eventually come around. They can't possibly bully and ostracize Sam forever.

*Knock on wood.*

I'm so tired of the stares and whispers. We are going to send a letter to all of our friends and family explaining that our child is transgender. Just think about it, what's the worse thing that could happen?

*Knock on wood.*

And as Sam got older, there was a new set of concerns to ward off...

I've spoken with a lawyer familiar with Judge Rosenbloom and he said she is fair. I know Sam is only 14 but I'm sure she'll grant our petition for a name change from Samantha to Samuel. How could she not?

*Knock on wood.*

Don't worry honey, I'm confident the TSA agent won't notice

that the name on the passport is Samuel but the gender marker is still an 'F.'

*Knock on wood.*

I called ahead and found they have a unisex restroom on the third floor of the museum right behind the dinosaur exhibit. If we confide in one of the field trip chaperones, I'm certain they will escort you there without the other kids finding out.

*Knock on wood.*

The full body security scanner at the airport can't see everything, right?

*Knock on wood.*

We are headed back a second time. There is no way we will get the same bigoted bitch at the Social Security Administration who refused to change his gender marker after pointing to Sam's crotch and asking if he had had surgery, "...down there."

*Knock on wood.*

He wouldn't really try to kill himself, would he?

*Knock on wood.*

Yes, I suppose you could say these three little words have become my daily devotion. A type of prayer for Agnostics like me to recite when ordinary situations most people take for granted become challenging. Common events such as being invited to birthday parties, using public restrooms and making friends, that don't come easily for my son Sam, merely because his mind and biology don't match. And so for what it is worth, I will continue uttering these words while at the same time tapping on the nearest piece of lumber (often times that being my head). Because I know in my heart that if I keep repeating this phrase, all of my worries and fears for my beautiful child will never come to be.

*Knock on wood.*

# AN APOLOGY FROM MY MIND TO MY BODY
*by Nikolas Martell*


When we were young
we were all  skateboard tricks
and bike races without hands,
hopscotch and secret hiding places.
We were a handmade kite catching the breeze;
bold expanse of fabric  we were seamless -
woven together, two of a kind, inseparable.
We bloodied our knees reaching for our sky,
broke bones and earned stitches,
understood perfection to be a childhood cocktail:
two parts daring and one part not knowing any better.
We drank up each day like we were the desert.

My body, forgive me.

My first mistakes were as innocent
as sippy cups, first shoes, safety scissors.
I swear, I never even knew I was a tailor
until I found myself holding the shears.
Now I cannot help but overlay your frame
with other people's measurements.
I imagine all the different ways I could dress you:
That skin tone. That body mass. That nose arch.
I no longer look at you in the mirror;
I do not want to see a work in progress.
I envision you four inches taller, voice deeper, hips smaller.
You are barely acceptable now, but you
you could be gorgeous.

My body, forgive me.

Each morning for breakfast I instruct you
to place the newspaper and toast upon the table,
set the knife with the sharp edge out.
You are always obedient, dutiful, temptation.
I do not have to stretch you out upon the gurney.

If I ask - if I *demand* - you will do it for me.
Use your hands to strap your body down.
Put on the vice grips.
Throw on the clamps.
Make the cuts as deep as I direct.
Pull yourself together with coarse thread.
Let the sutures slip in like sunshine.
This is how you make a body beautiful.

My body, forgive me.

I have made you into my own Frankenstein doll.
Monster, there are days I cannot tell love from horror.
Whole weeks I cannot look you in the eye.
Months that I avoid mirrors, windows, water...
everything that would show your reflection.
I cannot stand the sight of you,
of what you've let me turn you into.
I convince myself you did this, not me.
I am only the craftsman, the master.
You are the partner who never puts up a fight,
who will not leave me no matter what I do.
I want you to hate me, to hurt me back,
to make the fight more even.
But you will only ever love me,
remind me always that we are together
through sickness and in health
until death do us part.

My body, I am sorry.

I never agreed to that vow.
Never promised you the good life.
Never said I'd love you gentle.

This is not betrayal.
This is honesty.

## GREEN DRESS
*by Anonymous*

When I was little, I loved to run around the house in my mother's green dress and heels, until I was told that little boys couldn't wear dresses or heels. I would run around the house in circles, scuffing the kitchen floor, trying not to trip and fall as she ran after me. I was overcome with euphoria and panic at the same time, and started to believe that if I ran fast enough, I might slip through a portal or some sort of wormhole and be transported to a place where I could live as a girl. Instead, my mother caught up to me, grabbed me by the arm, stripped off the dress, scrubbed the red lipstick and blush off my face, and locked me out of her room. You might hate her. I certainly did.

She was terrified for me. Terrified of what people would do to me. She wasn't disgusted. She didn't think that she had failed. She needed time to figure it out. She needed time to understand. She researched, read books, went to support groups, slowly let me express myself any way I wanted to. First in the privacy of our home, and then beyond our safe walls. She was the first to call me "she", gave me fashion advice, and tips on shaving my legs. She even gave me that green dress a couple years ago.

I love you, mom.

# OUR TRUE SELVES

*by Erica & Patience Fields*

*Jennifer and Allison are on-stage, addressing the audience. Jennifer is 30s/40s, lesbian partner of Allison. Allison is 40s/ 50s, trans woman partner of Jennifer.*

ALLISON: It never would have occurred to me that falling in love would unlock so many doors that had eluded me about who I truly am. I thought that having surgery, and transitioning, would be all I would need and did not see that there was so much more to who I was until I fell in love with Jennifer.

JENNIFER: It never would have occurred to me that falling in love would open so many doors to places in my soul that I didn't even know existed. I was a self-assured lesbian, confident in my identity and my place in the community.

ALLISON: I always knew that I was a girl. I was caught at around 14 years old by my Mom with her lipstick on and she asked why I was wearing it. I just kept saying, "I don't know" until she let it go. I was terrified that she would figure it out so I buried my feelings so deep that no one would ever find out.

JENNIFER: At a very young age I understood my emotional desire to connect with girls before I even understood sex. When I finally had sex with a woman it solidified for me my place in life. I was a lesbian. I spent the next decade surrounded by women who loved other women. Other people in my life came and went... My lesbian status afforded me a close sisterhood, yet cost me meaningful connections with others who did not jump on the "lesbian cruiseship" with me.

ALLISON: In high school and college I lived as a guy, only occasionally being reminded of my truth. Those times were hard, but I found a way to cope with drugs. I kept hoping my feelings of not being who I truly should have been would go away, but they kept coming back. All along I had dated women, and had not thought anything of it. Maybe I really was just a heterosexual guy who had strange fantasies. I married and had kids and the feelings of being a woman went away, for a little while, but after a few years those feelings came back stronger than before. Then, after decades of keeping this secret from everyone, my wife caught me. She asked if the panties she found were some other woman's – terrified I'd been cheating on her – and I blurted out that they were... mine. There was silence. The truth was out. I told her everything, and she listened! We both cried and she asked me what was I going to do about it and I said, "I don't know." I began therapy and eventually decided to transition. I did it in record time, too – from bearded man in therapy to surgery in two years. I was finally together, confident and sure of myself. Finally in the right skin as the woman I'd always known I was.

BOTH: Then I met Allison/Jennifer.

JENNIFER: We connected immediately. Long conversations, shopping, mani-pedi's. I knew she used to be a guy. I was apprehensive. After a few months we found ourselves in San Francisco, a trip paid for by an overzealous bidding war at an industry auction. We spent every moment together, canvasing the city, holding hands, staring at the stars. I fell in love. How could I know that her past would change both of our lives.

ALLISON: When we fell in love on that trip to San Francisco, I was so smitten. For the first time in my life I loved a woman without any secret. I was honest. There was full disclosure and it felt amazing. We moved in together, and life became a couple thing. And with that comfort came some realizations: First, that I had never been heterosexual at all; I had been a lesbian all along, but trapped in a male body. Jennifer told me that I was just like any of the other partners she had been with over the years, and I was full of confirmation that I was truly the woman I had known myself to be. Sometimes communication was hard, as there were times that pieces of my past male character would surface – like a hiccup. Unexpected and startling. I would suddenly feel not myself, and Jennifer would help me see that it was understandable given my decades of male training. Becoming my true self is a process.

JENNIFER: It's been a few years since we first met. We are steadfast in our daily comings and goings, sharing a loft in the city and chores on the weekends. On the surface our relationship seems quite ordinary. Mundane even. Internally it is a constant stream of examining our perceptions. Perceptions of ourselves: who we are, and who we have been taught to be. Perceptions are not solid, they are fleeting. We have both been deeply conditioned to react to circumstances in a certain way. I learned not to fight within myself, but instead to see it for what it is... Conditioning.

ALLISON: If I could do it over again, I would transition as soon as I knew who I was. I missed out on everything a girl does and goes through when growing up - the good, the bad and the ugly. But without dwelling on what could have been, I am so happy to finally be me.

JENNIFER: Labels held their course for me for too many years – especially in those early years. When I learned to let it go, and focus on me, I found my freedom. Discovering, finding, being, and living as my true self is so liberating. I am so happy that Allison is her true self today, despite the occasional challenges, and that I am as well.

that. But that is not me. I can't help feeling disappointed that some people in the queer community want to assign behavior expectations ON to me. Since we are already breaking "the rules," I think we should be given the freedom to be who we truly are.

My wife is a mix of identities and presentations. She can rock a dress and tights and smoky eyes like nobody's business, or she can wear a black tank, show off her tats and sexy, strong arms, muscled clavicle, and pompadour, and equally bring me to my knees. And I love this. I am lucky to have found someone who confidently embraces her mix of genders and values how they manifest in her each day. I am constantly challenging my own gender assumptions and my fears that the queer community will take away my "butch" card because I am attracted to my girlfriend's masculinity. Or feel ashamed if I want to tell her that she drives me crazy when she wears lingerie. And I am conflicted because even though I did not register for my "butch" card, I am not prepared to fully give it up because of the afforded acceptances that come with it.

Complexity is often considered to be a feminine trait, and expecting butch women to not have stereotypically feminine qualities can cause disappointment, isolation, and rejection. For everyone. Challenging gender perceptions can be beautiful and painful. As I walk through my daily reality, I consistently make the conscious choice to ignore the erroneous perceptions and assumptions made by those around me and bravely, courageously strive to be who I am.

I would like to go back and tell my 11-year-old self that I married that gorgeous woman from my dreams this year. And that, yes, she kisses me. And touches me as I wrap my body around her and I love all of it. And that I'm still that sensitive tomboy who gets to wear boy's clothes. And cry. In her arms.

Oh, and I don't ever have to wear dresses on Sundays anymore. Unless I want to.

# BODY UNFOLDING
*by Charles Ely*


Suddenly reflected in all those eyes and even
                              the Cyclops eye of immortality
transforming your likeness into
            ones and zeros.
      You, now, able at once to be prosaic and worthy
            of admiration      of sexual attention      of affection.
And you want to see yourself in porn
            And you want to see yourself as the hero of an action flick
      And you want to see yourself as the president
                              of the United States of America
But today you would like to see yourself at all, settle
      for seeing yourself reflected back at you
when you look into the mirror.

LGBT: a definition
      Lesbian, Gay, ...whatever, the point is—
But I'm not sure what the point is.
This man likes to provoke politics,
            and he will share anything he has,      a "true Christian."
Why is love the sinner hate the sin one of the most cruel things
            ever done to me?
      How can he look up the statistics on lgbt teen suicide,
after I told him these equal rights you do not believe in
            fucking      matter, at least to these lost souls
            and then next time he protested he found only
the rise of all youth choosing death over this world, again, and
      again.
He says give them religion.
I say give them a world worth living in.
                                    A world
where most of the catastrophes of the last hundred years
      weren't done on purpose
                        and I wanted to say forget suicide.
Those people he does not even know the word for
      are the number one hate crime, dead
and I do not need something else for us to pretend isn't true.

Politics are not "just an opinion" –
they are a signed and sealed judgment on somebody else's life.
They are the state saying if you aren't white
     if you aren't straight if you aren't thin or rich or young or
               worst of all, if you aren't American –
   well I would say God help you, but you'll
     have to get your own God.
I won't tell him I'm trans –
I do not tell a lot of people I'm trans –
   because yes of course it's something I'm ashamed of,
                   that I do not have a penis.

See someone, anyone, needs to remember
  you can't love someone when you cut out half of who they are
    you can't love yourself when you cut out half of who you are
    and when you pretend whole demographics do not exist
    we are already gone before we are dead.

Read off that list of names
a memorial plaque
     the dead in a war
   none of them meant    to be fighting.
A war against that fear possessing like a monster
          moving through groups of people,
      twisting in their stomachs,
    the fear hardening into the need to
        hammer     home    a point
  whatever sharp edge that point takes and sometimes
all it takes
   is turning away.
       Paramedics who won't heal an "it" –
the Hippocratic Oath falls short this time. And that other time.
So.

Say Shaman, Two-Spirit. Otherize this journey
but do it the right way: call it courage.
I won't be your afterthought, tagged on in the space between
   the acronym and the point when someone sighs and says
        "alphabet soup."
Do those bodies up right, wash the blood away,
  and cover them in flowers

like the wishful thinking paintings of Ophelia.
Send them up bedecked
  as an Indian bride to a smiling God.
Push their boats into the sea
    and set them ablaze like Viking heroes.
Place gold coins over eyelids
    and let them cross the Styx.


    These customs all from community,
      from belonging,
    have a place to call home and someone
  to miss you when you're gone,
to place those coins on your eyelids
so you can pay the boatman.
So the mortician can dress up your body one more time,
deny mortality and that we are all made of meat.

But the customs for warzones are different –
    a whole life cremated and mourned in the bare
        syllables of a name.
Because everybody belongs somewhere. Believe that.

Maybe it is a kind of magic to say
    our bodies do not define us.
Our dead do not define us.
Our war does not define us.
Our gods do not define us.
Our loves do not define us.
We paint our own edges,
      and it is not war paint.
      It is transformation.

      It is art.

## *JUST DRAGGIN' ALONG*
*by Mykee Steen*

I have a winter coat of blue
It was made for a woman – something I knew
When I accepted it from my nice butch friend,
She was glad I took it, and I'd wear it to no end.
Though I generally have a manly build,
I fool many when that coat is filled
I never thought it was feminine to wear sky blue
For there ARE my eyes – yet a woman gave me those too.
One day I was walking, in the cold autumn bliss,
And I heard a woman say, "Uh, excuse me, miss!"
Seeing me closer she said "Sorry!"
as she asked where to find the train.
But I was complimented,
her apology was in vain.
Another time I was biking downtown,
trying to beat the red light.
And a woman yelled, "Oh, she's zooming!"
at someone in her sight.
As I turned my head,
I was the only biker to see.
I was the one zooming, honey,
I was,
Me.

## WHEN YOU WIGGLE LIKE THAT
*by Jes Versace*

i like it in the mornings, between the folds of blankets and
interlocking legs,
when the weight of your body falls into and embraces me from
behind-
when your fingertips find my thigh and your hand finds my ass
-tap tap smack -

when in the thick of night and bumps one too many
(~~or not nearly enough at all~~),
between the heavy and the banter, and the sound of a lighter
-flic..flick -

a slow, deep inhale of california grown
and the feel of, the touch of
the taste -
the taste of smokey and lips. lips and,
tobacco. and tobacco and herbs-
herbs.
and lips, full and thick. and thick and full beneath the scruff
and the very tips of all the hairs
that litter most every part of these gendered bodies
(genderedbodies)
and genderless souls.

The muscle, the muscle that ebbs and flows into the specific
curvature that defines your bicep
the tightening of your grip and the bite of your lip
the exhaled quiet whimper of a
groan,
that escapes your lips as hips
as hips absorb the heat,        -fire- like fire.

# A REQUIEM FOR THE QUEERS (OR WHY WE WEAR THE COLOR PURPLE)

*by Andrea Jenkins*

We wear purple because all Queens deserve a royal crown, because it speaks volumes to those who claim they are color-blind and it connects us to an ancient cultural legacy.

We wear purple because Marsha P. Johnson and Sylvia Rivera-two S.T.A.R. (Street Transvestite Action Revolutionaries) wore purple when they marched at Stonewall.

We wear purple for all the Queers who died on June 24th, 1973, in New Orleans when a bigoted homophobe sprayed Ronsonol lighter fluid on the stairs and tossed a match, and the ensuing flames travelled to the Upstairs Lounge killing 32 people, forty years ago, just four years after Stonewall.

We wear purple for all of the Queer, Trans and questioning youth that will sleep under a bridge, or trade sex for a place to stay tonight.

We wear purple for the indigenous two-spirit people, representing our struggle on the daily.

We wear purple because Radical Women of Color Feminism shapes our mindset and thought process, offering critical resistance to the prison industrial complex, male patriarchy, and religious subjugation.

We wear purple because we have to rewrite the narrative of what is and who is a woman.

We wear purple for all the kids bullied in school for taking the risk to be themselves.

We wear purple because the intersection of Race, Class, Gender and Sexuality is the street we live on, and we can't move even if we wanted to.

We have to act against what is considered normal- all of y'all can go and get married now, but I can't even vote because my identification doesn't match up with the person standing in the ballot box.

Y'all can get married now, but I still have to suffer a urinary tract infection because I can't go to the bathroom in some public places.

Y'all can get married now, but CeCe McDonald was locked up in the men's facility at St. Cloud Correctional Facility, for "standing her ground" against homophobic, transphobic, racist attacks, while George Zimmerman, who murdered Trayvon Martin is a free man walking around with a gun in his waistband.

Y'all can get married now, and I ain't mad at cha, in fact I am happy because it means we have moved a little closer to a more just, more righteous society, but we still got a long way to go.

The Personal is Political!

We wear purple for Miss Major and the Transgender Intersexed Justice Project, my home girl from Chicago, who marched at Stonewall, too, and is still putting in revolutionary work for the Trans brothers and Trans sistas on lockdown.

We wear purple for Leslie Feinberg and Kate Bornstein, two Transgender Warriors. We will never forget the lessons they've taught us about who we are, and what we are, and how beauty is our birthright, too.

I wear purple for my people, my beautiful Transgender people.

And what if love was the most powerful word in the ethos- Love, Love, Love, Love, - Love, Love, Love, Love, Love.

And what if my Transgender people were the embodiment of that Love?

Representing everything and nothing- We wear purple because Elton John sang:

"and you can tell everybody, this is your song, I know this might sound simple but, now that it's done. I hope you don't mind, I hope you don't mind, that I put down in the words, how wonderful life is when *queers* are in the world."

## CARPENTERS
*by Nikolas Martell*

When I came out as queer
I was welcomed out of the closet and into life,
as if I had not been living already.

Fuck the closet as a metaphor.

I do not come from laundry static,
clothes hangers, or worn out shoes.
I come from hate crimes on my street,
from too afraid to go to school
because last week the headlines were bloody.
I come from Stonewall, from protest and pride parade.
I come from every friend who loves me more for my honesty.

This closet - this altar of dust –
it cannot contain all that I am,
cannot hold all that we are.

We are fire in the soil
smoldering at the roots.
We teach timber:
it is no match for the fury of survival.

So fuck the metaphor.

The closet is nothing more
than dumb carpentry and dull hinges.
It is an illusion that blames the oppressed
for not opening the door and walking away.
It is a cheap magic trick that makes the "problem" disappear.
It is an easy excuse for every suicide.

We should give credit where it's due.
See, prejudice is a generous beast;
the more we ignore it the more it keeps giving.
So let us recognize the gift.

Put up a plaque for every carpenter.
List the names of each bigot and bully:
the Westboro Baptists, the Michele Bachmanns,
the teacher who still allows the word faggot in class.
Show them the closet for what it really is:
wood laid out 84 inches long, 28 wide.
A mahogany maw dressed in silk.
A coffin waiting for the earth.

These carpenters, these makers of caskets,
they are telling our stories for us,
stealing our love and locking it away.
As if static cling left razor blade bites
or clothes hampers held baseball bats.
Please, we come from deeper earth than that,
from six feet of other peoples bullshit
and slurs on our headstones.
We are the premature burials
that refuse to stay buried.
We are the kind of triumph
that carries dirt beneath its nails
and splinters in its teeth.

We will not always have the strength for pride.
The morning after the beating,
after the slur or death threat,
waking with mouths full of grime
we may want nothing more
than to tear down our signs,
retreat from the streets.

The carpenters will call this defeat,
as if living demands perfection,
as if survival were always pretty.
But our passion requires no such grace.
Let the carpenters champion their closets,
let them have even their caskets.
For there is no wood that does not burn
and we are nothing if not fire.

# ACT TWO

## *MIRRORS*
*by Sam Berliner, TJ Carley, and Tobias K. Davis*


*Imagine a locker room, where only transmasculine people go, and no cisgender men are allowed. Throughout the course of the piece, three transmasculine characters discuss (alone, to the mirror, to the audience, and/or to each other) their physical presentation, their perceptions of themselves, and the worlds' perceptions of them. They each stand before an imaginary mirror. They can be changing, inspecting their faces and bodies, getting dressed, getting undressed, getting ready, just arriving, anything, really. Perhaps they shave. Or groom. Or brush teeth, put on deodorant, squeeze pimples. Perhaps there are three sinks in front of the imaginary mirrors, or a locker room bench behind them, or behind each of them. Sam is the youngest. Toby has a beard. Sam should have some facial hair as well, if possible. TJ does not have any visible facial hair.*

*Lights up on Sam, alone – center stage right – addressing both the imaginary mirror in front of him, and the audience.*

SAM:   Who do I see when I look in the mirror? Scanning over creases and freckles. Cheekbones. Blue eyes. Jaw line. The angles and the soft spaces. Features that add up to who I have come to understand myself to be. I see the middle, in-between. I see genderqueer androgyny. I see myself.


*TJ enters the stage, and takes a spot opposite Sam – center stage left – and begins to investigate his face and hair – miming being in front of a mirror. Sam is aware that TJ entered – perhaps they share a glance or make eye contact.*

SAM: What about when you look? Who do you see? How can we both see the same thing but perceive something so completely different? And what will happen when our perceptions meld into one?

TJ: The mirror shows me that my forehead is growing wider by the day.

SAM: I am in a state of constant change. Hyper awareness, and voice cracks, and voice drops, and belly hair, and veiny hands, and achy changing muscles that leave me stretching every half hour.

TJ: I'm starting to see more of the top of my scalp than I care to, and I have completely stopped looking at the back of my head. I know what's back there; it's a thinning area, a region with less hair, the beginning of a potential comb-over. Okay, okay, it's a bald spot. My wife, God bless her, says bald men are sexy... I'm a short, round white man with hips. Add bald to that description and I'm definitely not sexy.

SAM: With each new physical change, I ponder the notion of "passing". This was not my intention. My comfortable androgyny is falling away. I am no longer read as female. No longer read as androgynous. In the search for alternatives I begin to realize that, however inadvertently, I have chosen the path of being seen as male. Exhilarating, but scary.

*As TJ continues, Toby enters and takes a spot between Sam and TJ – center stage– and begins to investigate his face and hair and body – miming looking into a mirror. Sam and TJ are aware that Toby has joined them – perhaps they all 'manly nod' to each other, make eye-contact, share an unspoken 'hello'.*

TJ: Remember puberty? *(Sam laughs to himself at the memory)* I got a training bra and became a chocolate-craved monster every month – what fun! Other girls obsessed over make-up and clothes, but I just wanted hair. I envied the boys – longed to be like them, with shadowy mustaches, dark, thick leg and arm hair, and beards. I loved it. I loved them. I wanted to be them. I wanted hair.

TOBY: *(in love with his current beard...)* I am not one of those trans men who has always longed for a beard. *(TJ rolls his eyes)* In fact, I swore I'd never grow facial hair at all. When I first started T, I was afraid of being stuck with four chin hairs, scraggly and awkward. But then I started to be able to grow more and more hair on my face, and over winter break one year I decided to see what would happen if I didn't shave. And poof! Hair! On my face! Bristly and coarse. To my surprise, I liked it. And my partner liked it. So it stayed. I think now I would feel naked without it.

SAM: Who do I see when I look in the mirror? Myself. Still. Yet different. A new version of myself? The same blue eyes peer back at me and the same ears just like my dad's. With slight differences. The soft spaces are rougher around the edges, the angles are more pronounced. Occasional facial hair, when I let it grow. Arm hair getting darker and more thick. Yet the more I stare, the more I still see that same person looking back at me. How is it, then, that everyone else has come to see me so differently than they did a year ago, when the changes that I perceive are so slight? Unconscious signifiers. Split-second-gendering. *(really looks at himself)* In their eyes I am so, unquestionably male.

TOBY: I thought it was just a fashion statement, but it has become so much more than that. This beard has become my armor as I move through the world. With a beard on my face I no longer fear that someone will think I'm a woman, no matter what I do, what I wear, or who I'm with. With this beard on my face I finally feel completely comfortable in the men's room. With this beard on my face I can wear bright colors, I can talk with my hands, I can giggle, which I do a lot, usually in a high pitched fashion.

TJ: At 35 years old, having come out as a transman, I was about to start puberty all over again. I eagerly anticipated the effects of testosterone – dreaming of a deep voice and 5 o'clock shadows. Seven years since my first shot of "T" and things are fine for the most part, but my follicles didn't get the memo. I have hair, more hair, but unfortunately and somewhat frighteningly, I have NO control over where it decides to grow. It started innocently enough on my belly. Cute and predictable. Then it spread to my legs and grew thick and dark. It has even crept up my chest. I remember running into the living room to show my wife the first five chest hairs that proudly adorned my otherwise bare chest. I'm so glad we didn't have company. But, my long-desired facial hair is still woefully missing in action.

SAM: You treat me like man but all the while the genderqueer on the inside is terrified. Frightened that you'll see through the mask, that you'll discover my unintentional secret and feel tricked, like the joke is on you. Can't you see me? I'm right here. My genderqueerness, my female past, is all right here in my face. Yet you don't see it. In my journey to congruity that part of me has become invisible. And This Is Terrifying.

TOBY: Yes, I am a man. And yes, I want you to treat me like a man. But how would you have treated me six years ago, before I had this beard? Would you have smiled at me then? Would you have called me by my name? Would you have called me he? I made it easy for you with this beard. I made it easy for me. I was tired of hard. Tired of correcting pronouns, of hating myself, of hating you. This beard means so much to all of us. It changes how you treat me. It changes how I treat you.

TJ: Every day I faithfully shave the 15 stubbles on my chin, just to humor myself. Every third day I'll swipe over the fuzz above my lip. And every few weeks, I'll break out the shaving cream...just because I have it (and have had it, since two Christmases ago when my wife gave it to me).

TOBY: I love how nice you all are to me now. You see a nice, nonthreatening, geeky guy who makes terrible puns and loves his poodle. And that's part of who I am. But not all of who I am. This beard hides my past. I know what it's like to fear men when I walk down the street. I know what it's like to have people scream at me WHAT ARE YOU? I also know what it's like to catch another queer's eye across the room. To know that we are not alone, that we have each other's backs; us against the world. I know what it's like to be a part of a rich web of deviant gender identities fighting together for our rights. I know what it's like to fight every day desperately to be seen as who I am.

SAM: To me, I am still androgynous. Still genderqueer. But somehow, you seeing MALE is closer to how I feel. Somehow, when all is said and done, you seeing MALE is precisely what I want you to see.

TJ: I guess I'm lucky... Despite little success in the facial hair arena, you all see me as male. Sure, there are parts of my body that still scream "woman!" - at least in my head sometimes, but you accept me, which is something I was afraid of for so long - acceptance, at just being who I am supposed to be.

TOBY: But really this beard is cosmetic. It's armor. It's an outer layer. It is a shortcut to my identity. It is me, but not all of me. It keeps me safe. It lets me be.

SAM: Slowly, this panic, this hyperawareness, this gender monitoring is quieting down. The constant buzzing in my head is now only a whisper. You may not see me how I see myself but you see me, finally, as the person I am presenting to you. And this perception, this commonality, this bridge is what has finally melded into one. This new sense of self, like warm liquid, fills my body and washes slowly over me, reminding me to breathe. *(pause)* Reminding me to just be.

# WORDS TO YOUNG QUEERS
*by Hannah Quinn Rivenburgh*

The politics of visibility mean that queer and trans ways of loving and of being most at home in our bodies carries within those acts certain risks. If we lived in a world free of homophobia and transphobia, this would not be the case. But instead, our bodies are familiar with that fear, that dis-ease.

Yet we are who we are in spite of all of that, and sometimes, in order to spite all of that. It means that our joys, our loves, our attractions, our visions, our fears, our declarations and definitions of beauty and strength and power and difference and truth have much at stake. Therefore it is crucial that we grasp deeply and hold closely that which is most strongly felt within us. In the words of Black lesbian feminist mother warrior poet Audre Lorde, "I feel, therefore I can be free." We must struggle not to lose sight of those parts of us which are most raw, most open, most generous, most hopeful. Most vulnerable. Queer ways of being and loving open up possibilities for us all.

I don't feel like anything more than one messy imperfect muddling person. I am, however, trying to thrive in community with others despite – and in order to spite – the forces which would see difference annihilated.

# MAKING CHANGES TO INCREASE GENDER IDENTITY CONGRUENCE: A ONE-PERSON EXPLORATION WITH THE TRANSGENDER CONGRUENCE SCALE

by G Zachariah White, MFA, PsyD

Congruence—to align, to match, to be in harmony. The Transgender Congruence Scale (TCS) developed by Dr. Holly Kozee (2008) is a measure of congruence between a person's gender identity and 3 areas—their appearance, their body comfort, and their sense of pride—over the preceding 2 weeks. The TCS provides an overall congruence score and 3 subscores reflecting the aforementioned areas of congruence. There is evidence supporting the instrument's validity and reliability. However, there have been no published data for reference groups.

As a genderqueer person and as a psychologist who works with transgender and other gender-nonconforming people, I took interest in the TCS. I developed a spreadsheet for scoring and graphing the results of the TCS. The scores are generated as an arithmetic mean of the answers given to each scale's questions. Thus, each of the 4 scales has a range from 1.0 to 5.0 with 1.0 being least congruent and 5.0 being most congruent.

I administered the TCS to myself to see what would show up. I recognized that my presentation at the time I first answered the questions fit within the social template of a male presentation. There was nothing in my presentation that expressed my queerness. I generally feel comfortable with my body, and I generally feel good about my gender identity.

The resulting scores were consistent with these self-observations. My lowest score was on the subscale of Appearance Congruence (2.8). My Body Comfort score (4.4) and my Gender Identity Pride score (5.0) were on the high end of the scale. My Total Congruence score was 3.6.

Faced with what seemed to be an Appearance Congruence deficit, I began to think about how I might raise that score. I have from time to time worn a pair of more feminine shoes; however, weather and style considerations mean that the shoes are not always suitable. I had the idea of painting one of my fingernails with nail polish as an expression of my gender identity, and this is what I did.

Over the following 2 weeks, with my painted fingernail, I observed how I felt. I noticed times when I wanted to hide my nail from view and times when I felt easy and open about my nail. I received a few questions about my nail, allowing an opportunity to disclose and discuss my gender identity. I received a few compliments on my nail, which left me feeling warm and seen.

After 2 weeks, I administered the TCS again, expecting to see an increase in the Appearance Congruence score and wondering how much it might have moved. My Appearance Congruence score increased from 2.8 to 3.8. My Body Comfort score (4.2) and my Gender Identity Pride score (5.0) were roughly unchanged. My Total Congruence score increased from 3.6 to 4.0.

Now I wonder what I might do to raise my Appearance Congruence score further. I wonder how my scores might compare with samples of genderqueer, transgender, and other gender non-conforming people. I would be curious to know how samples of cisgender people score. Clinically, I wonder if my process might provide a prototype for an intervention intended to increase gender identity congruence for others in the community.

Oh, and thank you, Dr. Kozee; I feel a bit more harmonious now.

### Reference

Kozee, H. B. (2008). The Development and Psychometric Evaluation of the Transgender Congruence Scale. (Doctoral dissertation). Retrieved from http://rave.ohiolink.edu/etdc/view?acc_num=osu1218220920.

# UPSIDE-DOWN, INSIDE-OUT

*by JamieAnn Meyers*

My wife and I were shopping for a reclining sofa at a furniture store, and when I sat across the desk from the salesperson to complete the purchase, they said:

"You must be Peggy."

"No, I'm JamieAnn."

"Oh, it says Peggy Meyers here in the previous sales records. So what's your last name?"

"Meyers."

"Oh.....? Oh!"

"Ok...here's how it is. Peggy and I were married as man and woman and I had a gender transition."

The salesperson abruptly leaned across the desk and said excitedly: "When did you have the surgery?"

*(pause)*

I took a deep breath and replied: "And how's your vagina today?"

Why is it that when someone discovers you are trans, they assume that you've had "the surgery?" First of all, what is "the surgery?"

Well, it must be all about your genitals, right?
I mean, it's obvious.

If you're a woman, you must have a vagina; and if you're a man, you must have a penis. Everybody knows this, right?

But think of the possibilities. If you're a woman and you have a penis, does this mean that you are both man and woman? Or either? Or neither? Or sometimes one, sometimes the other? Or someone else entirely?

*(sigh)*

We've come a long way, but we still have a lot of work to do. For me, the best way to educate people is to raise awareness by being out and sharing my story.

My friends say that I'm an attractive woman.
My skin is soft and smooth,
My breasts are full, and my hips and butt are gently rounded.
I'm gentle, and kind. I lead with my smile and I love people.

My doctor treats me as a post-menopausal woman...
with an oversized clit.
I love my clit! She's so sensitive!
I love to please her with my battery-operated girlfriend.
She's at the top of my inside-out vagina.

You see, I'm a woman born with an "outie."
My close friends say: "Oh my! It looks like a little penis!"
I identify as woman, always have, probably always will.
I live my life in my true identity, and my vagina is inside-out.

Some day, when it's time to "come out" to my five-year-old grandson as a woman with a transsexual history, I will tell him: "Some boys have vaginas, and some girls have penises."

And he will understand.

# FUCK STEREOTYPES
*by Love, Femme*

*Lights up on Femme, addressing the audience (and Butch at the same time). Butch is onstage, at a breakfast cafe table - frozen with a pecan roll or drinking coffee and reading the paper or something until engaged in the dialogue of the scene. Lighting should definitely be different when Femme is addressing the audience versus when Femme and Butch are talking.*

FEMME:  Dear Butch,

Although your friendship is so dear to me, you really fucking pissed me off this morning. Not just with the words you spoke, but also your ignorance behind them.

If I was wearing my cargo shorts and HRC t-shirt you would have never uttered such bullshit. But, I'm wearing a causal cotton dress and wedges today. Little did I know I was prime to be picked on. This conversation is how we both started our day. Over coffee and sticky pecan rolls. I agreed to crawl out of bed at an ungodly hour and meet you for breakfast. You smelled of cheap vodka and pussy still after spending all night with some random lady you had met at the bar. I came to hear you brag about your kinky adventures, not to be bitch slapped with stereotypes.

*(scene shift - from monologue to dialogue between Butch and Femme)*

BUTCH:  You know, she looked like a lesbian.

FEMME:  And, amuse me please, what does a lesbian look like?

BUTCH: Lean muscular build, short spiky hair, and threads right out of American Eagles men's section. Just a regular looking lesbian.

FEMME: Well, if that is the case then I must not be a "real lesbian" because I look nothing like that.

BUTCH: You could work a little harder on fitting in, just being honest.

*(OMG "is this for real" pause... returns to audience - or perhaps stands up and says all of this to Butch, but Butch does not hear or is not listening?)*

FEMME: I have curves and long hair.
My nails are painted.
I wear dresses from small independent stores
that cater only to plus size woman.
And, I am really fucking gay.
Like, super-duper fucking gay.
As queer as they come, with a cherry on top.
Even in lacy undergarments, fancy dresses, ridiculously tall heels,
Adele-inspired eyeliner, and pouty glossy lips I am still really ... truly ... incredibly ... fucking ... gay. Fuck the box you are trying to put me in. Fuck stereotypes. Fuck you.

*(subtle Femme exit... might swat her own hair on her way out... )*

FEMME: Love,
Femme

# TRUE THINGS I DON'T SAY
*by Galen D. Smith*


True things I don't say:

I don't love my body.
I feel at least as much shame about not loving my body as I do about my body itself.

I really, really want to be fat positive. I think fat queers are hot. Other fat queers.
I weigh myself most days. I feel good when I weigh less. I feel bad when I weigh more.
Then I feel bad about feeling bad.

I talk about being disabled all the time. I am a disability justice leader.
I say "I'm disabled and proud!"
I talk a lot about creating access for other disabled people.
I don't talk about how my learning and psych disabilities make it hard to be in community.
I don't talk about how the way my brain works can make it look like I'm a loud, obnoxious, uncommitted, white guy who is unaware of his privilege and how much space he's taking up.
I don't talk about how my shame makes it hard to imagine what access looks like for me.

I stopped taking testosterone, for a year.
I was afraid to tell anyone.
I bled every month.
I still don't know why I did it.

When someone asks me "How did you know you were trans?" I want to say, "I didn't know for sure and sometimes I still don't".
I never say that.

I am a really privileged person who is using my privilege in a way that gives me even more privilege.
I know it's important to recognize that.

Most days I have no idea what I'm supposed to do about it.

It felt ridiculous to voluntarily go to a hospital and ask someone to cut off a healthy part of my body.
I did it anyway, and I'm glad I did.

Knowing that people look up to me makes me very, very nervous.

*(pause... exhale)*

These are my truths. The ones I don't say out loud.

Until now.

# NO WORDS
*by Sarah James*

*Speaker is cisgender woman, perhaps telling the story on one side of the stage, in drag and already dressed as described in the piece, while on another part of the stage, her partner (cisgender male) – slowly gets dressed for the evening. Perhaps they help each other get ready. Perhaps they embrace, or dance, or get hot and physical. Or perhaps she is alone. You decide.*

We're getting dressed for the party.

The three dollar black bra we giddily bought at 6pm tonight is snug around his ribs, little balloons of rice already wedged in its lacy cups. He's pulling on the magenta suede skirt I bought forty pounds ago. Remembering how slick the lining felt against my bare thighs, how the weight of the leather tugged against the straps of my garter, I can't help but glide my hands down over his hips, snagging the hem and giving it a little slide, up, down.

We are utterly silent; his eyes go wide behind studious glasses. He wets his lips, and I can see the front of the skirt strain out as he hardens just that little bit. He isn't tucking and taping – we are what we are, after all, and control top hose are the best we can do, impromptu as we've been in this.

I can't keep my hands off, but I'm careful not to clasp or hold him in my hand, instead I stroke as I would a clit, with light fingers and circling spirals. We're in a bit of a frenzy then, kissing and rubbing, and I want nothing more than to step into the closet and pull on my disco-sparkle harness with the night black shaft already hung and hard for fucking.

Yet... we both pull back. There is something more important than sex going on, something bigger than bedroom games.

I finish pinning the stuffed sock in my BVDs, wrap my torso round and round and round until tits crush to meet belly and I am one smooth line under my t-shirt. Motorcycle boots lace up tight, and I've got my swagger on now.

We French braid his long spider-silk hair. It's so soft it immediately falls a bit, wisping around his face as I apply the blush. We can't agree on shadow color, so he gets to pick it out for her eyes.

There are no words for us to explain the tension that sings between us, to describe what is happening right now, not "alchemy", not "blurring" – those terms don't fit this streetlight starry night where it's right to go out as we are, to travel on the thrill and the edge of danger.

We climb in the car. Halfway there, we realize we have no names for each other, like this. We try on a few, but find none that match us. We pull up – nameless, damp-palmed, and blushing faces. I slip around the car to open the door and hand her out. One long smooth leg out the door, and then the other, like a starlet ready for the paparazzi. I waft my palm to the small of her back as she steps up onto the curb. Then we're practically running to the door. She glances sidelong at me and smiles with lips closed and his familiar, perverse twinkle dancing in her eyes. I gasp and feel my sock press tight against my pubic bone under brass zipper and denim. I lean in as we hit the door – a quick kiss, and I lick the bitter bubblegum of her glossy lips. She squeezes my hand. We pay our ten bucks to enter a land of freedom, a place where Adam's apples and breadths of hips are not the whole story, where everyone can move into (and out of) the truebeing, the daring experiment, or the fucked up dot on the continuum, whatever it ends up being for each of us tonight.

We dance. Sweet, downcast, through-the-lashes-glances bely every beating she got at thirteen, every lash of the tongue from her dad at fourteen, every heroin high that let her out for awhile, every hour and day she had to be *tough*.

She is so natural and soft. Her shoulders are down, hips loose and swinging as we close together. I swear I'm growing chest hair just looking at her. I've been a boy in public before, but

I've never seen her like this. That's it exactly; I haven't seen *her* at all, except in glimpses, in half-confessional role-play sex. And here she is – pressed tight against my chest, hips grinding against my crotch to the bass bump of the music. Her thigh along mine is electric heaven. Two drag queens cannot decide whether we are breeders or in drag. I stroke my mascara-made mustache at them – but none of it matters with my hands in suede and the way she smiles.

We break for bad punch and lukewarm beer, perusing the bake sale goods and patting sweat off our faces and necks. Back on the dance floor we smile too much again, helium bliss and elbows bumping with our temporary clan. When we finally stagger home, footsore, with strangled chests, there's nothing left for the erotic part of this as we topple down to sleep. We let go of the night. There are no words to explain this tension.

# AND DON'T CALL ME MA'AM
*by Alyx J. Hanson*

What can I get for you, sir?
I mean, ma'am?
I mean, sir?
I mean.......sorry?

Look, honey. I know you're only trying
to be polite.

But will you please stop trying to put me in a box
and just let me order my fucking burrito?

A fellow barista once asked me
if I had ever gotten into it
with a customer (or anyone)
for calling me "ma'am."

I said no.
He asked why not.

I told him it was because I shouldn't need
to defend my identity
to every customer in the drive-thru.

Because I shouldn't feel obligated
to explain my existence
to every bartender, or cashier,
or stranger on the street (or in the bathroom),
or to you.

I don't fit in boxes. My wingspan is too wide.

So do us both a favor.
Stop with your assumptions,
and I'll bring none of mine.

Perhaps we'll see each other more clearly without them.

## *ASK ME*
*by Alex Jackson Nelson*

Ask me what it means to be a trans guy.

If – or when I tell you –
will it be the same answer that other trans guys give you?
Will I feel as alone in my identity, my reality, and my understanding of the world as you, or you, or them?
Will sharing the information empower me? Make me less lonely? Will it make you see me?

All in comparison.

My rights are in comparison to my privilege.
My gender identity and expression
are in comparison to the broader queer community.
My sex life is in comparison to men born with penises.
My safety is in comparison to those less fortunate
(mainly, those with breasts really,
no matter their gender identity).
My family acceptance is in comparison to those who have been banished from their families.

Maybe the comparison makes it lonely.

Hey.
Ask me what it means to be a trans guy.
To have privilege and power.
To be white. To be able-bodied. To be strong.
To have the ability to hold someone down,
and to pick them back up.
A glance, a look – no recognition.
The thrill, the sorrow.
To walk down the street unnoticed while watching my trans sisters and fabulous genderqueer friends get beat down. To watch them watching me in fear.
I am the threat.

All in comparison.

**56**

DON'T YOU KNOW ME!?
My story, my life, my struggles, my fear.
Surrounded by so many people, and still so lonely.
Can you see me? Do you know what I have been through?
Or done for this community?

Tired. Lonely. And unseen.
All in vibrant community.

*(pause)*

Whose community?

# HE CALLS ME "MAMA"

*by Zealot Hamm*

It's five thirty in the morning. My son, almost two and a half years old, informs via the baby monitor that it's time to drag my sorry, misshapen carcass out of bed. At that hour, most adults are enjoying a good night's rest. How I miss that...

His mother tries to get up but I inform her that it's my turn. She mumbles and puts her face back into the pillow, waving me away, with her hand like an eager seal flipper – a common gesture for telling me, "fine, take care of it and please get away from me – your morning breath smells like hot garbage."

I put my house coat on and even though my legs don't support me at first, they somehow get it together enough so I don't hit the floor. I do my drunken dance of steps towards my son's room, open the door, and there he is: standing up in his crib, holding his stuffed monkey, and wide awake.

"Mama!" he exclaims.

A thousand fireflies light up in my heart.

He reaches for me. I pick him up and he lays his sleepy head on my chest, the familiar spot where we share a sacred space. It is a world that is made complete by little eyes that look back at me like the reflection of a magic mirror. I try real hard not to think of the future and all of the questions he will have once he understands the complex nature of my world. Will he hate me? Will he get mad me? Will he be resentful that in his world I am his mom, but to others I would be labeled his dad? I try not to think about it. I try not to let those thoughts and the acidic words of society get me down and make me feel less than a woman. I try not to let that world creep in and taint our private early morning paradise... But it is early, and I'm only human. Besides, this is not just about me.

This is about his future. Life has so much to offer, and I don't want him to look at me when he is older with those same brown eyes, those eyes that look to me for nourishing hugs and kisses, and say, "Why did you do this to me?"

I've read the heart wrenching stories of children of transgender parents and I know what happens when they fail. Children who can no longer look at, be around, or deal with their parent's transition and just... erase them. No phone calls. Pictures of parents cut up or thrown in the trash. Erased. Forgotten.

People don't understand. They don't understand my paralyzing fear. If I screw this up, I not only fail as a mother in my own eyes, but I fail as a human being before the world. As if that's not enough, I become another weaponized statistic that will be thrown at other parents who are trans. "See? I told you it wouldn't work. Now look..."

I can't imagine being separate from my son. Never holding his hand again. Or a future where I would never walk with him in the park or hear his voice talking to his friends on the phone. Being trans means taking a risk, but when you're trans and also a parent, it's like gambling blind with the most precious piece of your heart and every second the odds are stacked against you.

Before I can mentally go any further down that road, my son's voice pulls me back.

"Mama! Mama!"

Those words echo throughout my being and the force that held me back from this moment dissipates into the dark corners of my mind. I realize that, in this imperfect world full of danger and possibility, children do not ask you to be perfect. They just need you to love and care for them. To be good.

I cannot predict the future, nor can I make promises for a desired outcome that may never be. What I can do is try and not give up. I can try to be the best parent I can possibly be.

I finish putting on his fresh diaper and pick him up. He looks at me seriously and just as I am about to place him in his crib, he closes his eyes, as if concentrating on a really hard math equation.

"Mama?" he asks.

"Yes, baby?" I reply.

We sit there in silence for a moment, and then I hear it.

And then I smell it.

And a few seconds later we are both laughing hysterically! In his own little gassy way, I felt like he was showing me love, and trust, and though I may be the parent that no one expected for him to have, he calls me "Mama", and that's all I'll ever need.

# ASTERISK*

*by Oliver Renee Schminkey*


Dear asterisk,
the first time I saw you next to the
word 'trans*', I searched
for an explanation.  I searched
for an exception, for the rules
to follow.  You are mostly used like a footnote.  I see
the star, and my eyes jump to the bottom
of the page.  It's how I learn
the details of a contest or that the batteries
are not included or the fact that an author
has chosen to change all the names. You were
supposed to give me more information. Supposed
to tell me how to win the prize
or that I wasn't even eligible.

Dear person of potential significance,
I'm Oliver.  I'm genderqueer.  This means
(and you almost always have to explain
to people what this means), this means
that I don't identify on the gender binary.  I'm
an in-betweener.  I'm like a...liger; not quite a lion
and not quite a tiger, but probably still
the coolest fucking cat that ever lived.

Genderqueer means that I'm forced
to get good at explaining myself.  Genderqueer means
that I'm not allowed to feel comfortable taking a piss.  It means
I am not gay as in 'happy'; I am
queer as in 'fuck you.'  It means that strangers feel entitled
to ask about my genitals.  Genderqueer means
people are never quite certain, exactly
how *do* we have sex?

It means we are a question mark.  We are an asterisk
bearing no explanation.  We are whatever happens
when you mix hydrogen with oxygen and somehow get
this thing called water.  All it takes is one hurricane

to destroy entire cities, and we are oceans
spilling miles deep.  Science has not yet discovered one-tenth
of the creatures we hold within our seas. Just think
of our potential.

Dear cisgender people,
When I walk into bathrooms designed for you,
does it make you uncomfortable?  If it does,
then we are on the same fucking page.
I am only a tightrope walker searching
for the moment of balance between being comfortable
and refusing to hate my body.  So let's talk about
your women's sign, that stick person who
always wears that ridiculous fucking cape.

Dear triangle-bodied bathroom sign,
you are not a superhero.  Policing
my gender is not a legitimate career choice.

If you make sure everyone is the
same, that's supposed to make us feel comfortable
right?  But for a lot of transgender people, walking
into a bathroom is like choosing which side of the Civil War
they're fighting for.  Which relatives they'll have to shoot.

Genderqueer means that I don't even have a gun.
I have no promise of a transition, no promise that
one day, my body will match me, that other
people will see me for who I am.  Walking
into a bathroom for me is like
a one person hide and go seek.  No one's trying to
find me, but I always still feel like I'm hiding.

Some days, I'm jealous
of my partner who gets asked by rude strangers
"Are you a boy or a girl?" and they have
the opportunity to reply with 'neither.' Even with
my daddy's body hair, and a pretty solid
mustache, might I add, my body is still too much
curve to confuse people enough to ask.  Even when
the binding gives me backaches and I replace

half my wardrobe, I know that I will never
be passable without surgery or hormones. But
passable as what? "Are you a boy or a girl?" "Neither."

Sometimes I think it would be easier if I lied. If I just
picked 'man' or 'woman,' but this is not an option
for me. I could tell people I exist as
the shoreline or the rock bed but I will always be
a current running both ways. This fluidity
does not help me fit into small places. The water
in my blood betrays me every time.

Genderqueer means explaining myself, even to the queer
community. It means reminding the LGB that
the T isn't just tacked on as an afterthought. It means
defending my place on the spectrum, clinging to the
indigo in that rainbow. It means telling people to
fucking Wikipedia the meaning of the asterisk. It means
meeting with professors before class
to determine how to refer to myself in Spanish. My professor
tells me it is a language built on a binary romance, words
ending in -o for men and -a for women, and there are
no words to describe me. I do not find this romantic.
Genderqueer means that in most languages,
I do not even exist.

When people ask me
why I bind, I don't know what to tell them. My breasts
are not the enemy, and I know that I am lucky enough to love
my body despite the dysphoria. But for me, the binding
isn't just a piece of cloth; it's a yarmulke, it's
a priest's robes, it's every bible carried
in someone's pocket. It's the only thing that gives me hope
that someone will be confused enough to ask my
pronouns. And that is something sacred.

They say the body is a temple. But even temples
sometimes need a little remodeling. The body
is less like a holy dove and more
like a pigeon, more scavenger than savior. More
adaptation than preparation. But adaptation takes too

much time; evolution is a slow creature. We are puddles that
have not yet raged into tsunamis. In thirty-one states, it is
still legal to be fired based on gender expression. In
twenty states you can still lose your job
over your sexual orientation. So god forbid
we have to pee in Alabama. And please
don't fall in love in Mississippi or Tennessee. And if
you feel the need fight your dysphoria, dear god
you better not live in Louisiana or Utah
or Idaho West Virginia Wyoming
South Carolina North Dakota Oklahoma Florida
Georgia          Texas.

It is so bad that almost half of us decide
it is better not to live at all.

Dear schools that teach "tolerance",
I refuse to be merely tolerated. Remember
that we have the power to be tsunamis. In the
alphabet soup of our queer identity, we
deserve nothing less than a celebration. So let's
throw a party for our mustaches or lack thereof. For
every binder that fits too tightly. For every makeup smear
and five o'clock shadow. For plaid button up shirts
and bowties. For every girl who's told me that
my armpit hair is sexy. For the feel of skin
against skin. For that one barista who doesn't
gender me, from whom I will
probably buy another cup of tea.

For every shaking thirteen-year-old talking to
their father. For every person too afraid to come
out until they are twenty, or forty. For all the people
who come out anyway. For all who built
a community for me to stand in. For Laverne
Cox, for Sylvia Rivera, for Marsha P. Johnson. For everyone
who makes me feel as if this is actually a community. For
every person who gets my pronouns right. But really,
for every person who cares enough about me
to get my pronouns right. There's
a reason we have our own parade.

So let's celebrate the mornings we wake up
too tired for pride.  Those days where taking a shower
feels more like getting caught in the rain. Remember
that water makes things grow. Remember
that drowning is only breathing in
air that hasn't quite vaporized yet; we just
don't have the right lungs for it yet.  But
evolution is coming and god damn
if I'm not still alive when it does.

## End of Play

## Helpful Terms

**Assigned Sex At Birth:** At birth, infants are assigned a sex based on a combination of bodily characteristics including chromosomes, hormones, internal reproductive organs, and genitals.

**Cis/Cisgender:** The opposite of transgender – someone who identifies today as the sex they were assigned at birth.

**FTM (Female-to-Male):** A person assigned female sex and feminine gender at birth who is either transitioning into a male identity and/or body, or who identifies as a FTM trans person, trans man, or transsexual. As with any of the descriptive terms found here, never apply this label to a person without their express permission.

**Gender:** We define gender as a system of meanings and symbols and the rules, privileges and punishments for their use. All the ways in which people express their bodies and communicate with the world can be gendered and encoded with meaning—for example: vocal inflection, body hair, clothing, laughter, sexuality, and the very space one takes up in a room.

**Gender Binary:** The system that rigidly divides gender into the two categories of male and female (or masculine and feminine).

**Gender Expression:** The external representation of one's gender identity, usually expressed through feminine or masculine behaviors, and signals such as clothing, hair, movement, voice or body characteristics.

**Gender Identity:** One's internal sense of who they are; being a woman or man, girl or boy, or between or beyond these genders.

**Gender Identity Disorder (GID):** A controversial DSM-IV diagnosis given to transgender and other gender-variant people. Because it labels people as "disordered", Gender Identity Disorder is often considered offensive. The diagnosis is frequently given to children who don't obey expected norms in terms of dress, play or behavior. Such children are often subjected to intense psychotherapy, behavior modification and/or institutionalization. This replaces the outdated term "gender dysphoria".

**Gender Variant/Gender Non-Conforming:** A person who does not conform to gender-based expectations of society (including transgender, transsexual, intersex, genderqueer, cross-dresser, etc.) As with any of the descriptive terms found here, never apply this label to a person without their express permission.

**Genderqueer:** A person whose gender identity is neither male nor female, is between or beyond genders, or is some combination of genders, in terms of expression and/or identity. As with any of the descriptive terms found here, never apply this label to a person without their express permission.

**MTF (Male-to-Female):** A person assigned male sex and masculine gender at birth who is either transitioning into a female identity and/or body, or who identifies as a MTF trans person, trans woman, or transsexual. As with any of the descriptive terms found here, never apply this label to a person without their express permission.

**Pronouns:** A replacement word for the subject – she/her, he/him. Some transgender or gender non-conforming individuals choose to use gender-neutral pronouns such as they/them or ze/hir.

**Queer:** An umbrella term often used by people to refer to their own gender identity and/or sexuality in a way that is far less limiting than the gender binary or the "LGB" part of the popular acronym. "Queer" includes anyone who a) wants to identify as queer and/or b) who feels somehow outside of the societal norms in regards to gender, sexuality, and/or politics. Depending on the user, the term may have either a derogatory or an affirming connotation, as many have sought to reclaim the term that was once widely used in a negative way. As with any of the descriptive terms found here, never apply this label to a person without their express permission.

**Transgender:** An umbrella term for people whose gender identity and/or expression differs from the gender they were assigned at birth or from what is culturally validated. Trans people choose many words to describe themselves and/or their communities, including but not limited to: transsexual, genderqueer, Two Spirit, FTM, MTF, drag queen or king, cross dresser, gender non-conforming, gender variant, woman, and man.

**Trans\*:** When you see "trans\*" in print, this shortened, asterisked word generally refers to a group of people that includes transgender and gender non-conforming individuals.

**Transition:** Refers to the complex process of altering one's gender, which may include some, all or none of the following: changing name and/or sex on legal documents; hormone therapy; and chest, facial and/or genital alteration. Transgender people may or may not choose to alter their bodies.

**Transsexual:** A person whose intent is to live as a gender other than that assigned at birth. Most transsexuals engage in some process of altering either primary or secondary sexual characteristics, through hormone treatment or surgery or both. Some transsexuals live full time in their chosen gender without any alteration to physiology. As with any of the descriptive terms found here, never apply this label to a person without their express permission.

**Transphobia:** The fear and hatred of or the discomfort with people who identify or may be perceived to be transgender, respectively. Transphobic reactions often lead to intolerance, bigotry, and violence against anyone not perceived to match gender norms. Transphobia is not homophobia, yet they do have a connection. Stereotypes of the lesbian and gay communities are often based on gender expressions and/or roles within a binary gender system in a monosexual (hetero, gay, lesbian) paradigm (i.e. gay men as effeminate, lesbians as masculine, etc). Since trans-identified folks transgress a binary gender system, they may be more susceptible to homophobic actions.